TALES OF MYSTERY AND IMAGINATION

Imagine you are in an old house by a lake. It is night and there is a wild storm outside, the wind screaming around the grey stone walls. Far below the house, in a gloomy vault, lies the dead body of the Lady Madeleine in her coffin. In the room with you is her brother, looking at you with wild, mad eyes. Imagine this . . . and you are in the House of Usher.

Turn the page, and a Black Cat is hanging by its neck from a tree. Turn another, and you will hear music as a thousand people sing and dance at a wonderful masked ball. You are now in the castle of Prince Prospero. Inside, all is light and life and pleasure, but outside the castle walls walks the terrible masked figure of the Red Death . . .

These stories will take you into the shadowy world of the imagination, into a land of terror and dreams and madness.

Don't read them alone!

D0206761

OXFORD BOOKWORMS LIBRARY

Fantasy & Horror

Tales of Mystery and Imagination

Stage 3 (1000 headwords)

Series Editor: Jennifer Bassett
Founder Editor: Tricia Hedge
Activities Editors: Jennifer Bassett and Alison Baxter

EDGAR ALLAN POE

Tales
of Mystery
and Imagination

Retold by
Margaret Naudi

OXFORD UNIVERSITY PRESS

OXFORD
UNIVERSITY PRESS

Great Clarendon Street, Oxford OX2 6DP

Oxford University Press is a department of the University of Oxford.
It furthers the University's objective of excellence in research, scholarship,
and education by publishing worldwide in

Oxford New York

Auckland Cape Town Dar es Salaam Hong Kong Karachi
Kuala Lumpur Madrid Melbourne Mexico City Nairobi
New Delhi Shanghai Taipei Toronto

With offices in

Argentina Austria Brazil Chile Czech Republic France Greece
Guatemala Hungary Italy Japan Poland Portugal Singapore
South Korea Switzerland Thailand Turkey Ukraine Vietnam

OXFORD and OXFORD ENGLISH are registered trade marks of
Oxford University Press in the UK and in certain other countries

This simplified edition © Oxford University Press 2008

Database right Oxford University Press (maker)

First published in Oxford Bookworms 1993

14 16 18 20 19 17 15 13

No unauthorized photocopying

All rights reserved. No part of this publication may be reproduced,
stored in a retrieval system, or transmitted, in any form or by any means,
without the prior permission in writing of Oxford University Press,
or as expressly permitted by law, or under terms agreed with the appropriate
reprographics rights organization. Enquiries concerning reproduction
outside the scope of the above should be sent to the ELT Rights Department,
Oxford University Press, at the address above

You must not circulate this book in any other binding or cover
and you must impose this same condition on any acquirer

Any websites referred to in this publication are in the public domain and
their addresses are provided by Oxford University Press for information only.
Oxford University Press disclaims any responsibility for the content

ISBN 978 0 19 479132 8

A complete recording of this Bookworms edition of
Tales of Mystery and Imagination is available in an audio pack ISBN 978 0 19 479314 8

Printed in China

Typeset by Wyvern Typesetting Ltd, Bristol

ACKNOWLEDGEMENTS
Illustrated by: Ian Miller

Word count (main text): 11,960 words

For more information on the Oxford Bookworms Library,
visit www.oup.com/elt/gradedreaders

CONTENTS

The Fall of the House of Usher

It was a grey autumn day and the sky was full of large black clouds. All day I had ridden through flat and uninteresting countryside, but at last, as it began to grow dark, I saw the end of my journey.

There, in front of me, stood the House of Usher. And at once – I do not know why – a strange feeling of deep gloom came down on me and covered me like a blanket. I looked up at the old house with its high stone walls and narrow windows. I looked around at the thin dry grass and the old dying trees, and an icy hand seemed to take hold of my heart. I felt cold and sick, and could not think of one happy thought to chase away my gloom.

Why, I wondered, did the House of Usher make me feel so sad? I could find no answer.

There was a lake next to the house and I rode my horse up to the edge and stopped. Perhaps from here the house would not seem so sad, so full of gloom. I looked down into the mirror of dark, still water, and saw again the empty, eye-like windows of the house and the dying trees all around it. The feeling of gloom was stronger than ever.

It was in this house that I was going to spend the next few weeks. Its owner, Roderick Usher, had been a good friend of mine when I was a boy. I had not seen him for many years, but recently he had sent me a letter – a sad and terrible letter. He wrote that he was ill, ill in body and ill in mind; that he wanted and needed to see me. I was his only friend, the only

I looked down into the mirror of dark, still water.

person who could help him in his illness.

Although we had been good friends when we were young, I knew very little about him. He had never spoken much about himself, but I knew that he came from a very old family of which he was the last living man. I also knew that in the Usher family there had never been many children and so for hundreds of years the family name, together with the family home, had passed straight from father to son.

As I stood by the lake, my feeling of gloom grew and grew. I knew also that underneath my gloom lay fear, and fear does strange things to the mind. I began to imagine that the gloom was not in my mind, but was something real. It was like a mysterious cloud, which seemed to come straight from the dark lake and the dying trees and the old walls of the house. A heavy grey cloud, which carried with it disease and fear.

This was a dream, I told myself, and I looked more carefully at the building in front of me. It was, indeed, very old and I noticed that every stone had cracks and holes in it. But there was nothing really wrong with the building. No stones were missing. The only thing that I noticed was a very small crack which started at the top of the building and continued all the way down into the dark waters of the lake.

I went up to the front of the house. A servant took my horse and I stepped into the large hall. Another servant led me silently upstairs. On the walls there were many strange, dark pictures which made me feel nervous. I remembered these pictures from my earlier visits to the house when I was a child. But the feelings that the pictures gave me on this visit were new to me.

On the stairs we met the family doctor. He had a strange look on his face, a look that I did not like. I hurried on, and finally the servant opened a door and took me into the study.

The room was large and long, with high narrow windows, which let in only a little light. Shadows lay in all the corners of the room and around the dark pieces of furniture. There were many books and a few guitars, but there was no life, no happiness in the room. Deep gloom filled the air.

When Usher saw me, he got up and welcomed me warmly. I thought he was just being polite, but as I looked into his face, I could see that he was pleased to see me. We sat down, but he did not speak at first, and for a few moments I watched him in surprise and fear. He had changed so much since our last meeting! He had the same pale thin face, the same eyes, large and clear, and the same thin lips and soft hair. But now his skin was too white, his eyes too large and bright, and he seemed a different man. He frightened me. And his long wild hair looked like a ghostly cloud around his head.

I noticed that my friend was very nervous and that his feelings changed very quickly. Sometimes he talked a lot, then he suddenly became silent and did not say a word for many hours. At other times he found it difficult to think, and his voice was heavy and slow, like the voice of a man who had drunk too much.

He told me why he had wanted to see me, and how he hoped to feel better now that I was with him. He had, he explained, a strange illness which had been in his family for a long time. It was a nervous illness which made him feel everything much more strongly than other people. He could only eat food that was almost tasteless. He had to choose his clothes very carefully because most of them hurt his skin. He could not have flowers in his room because their smell was too strong for him. Light hurt his eyes, and most sounds hurt his ears – except the soft sound of guitars.

Worst of all, he was a prisoner of his own fear. 'I shall

die,' he used to say, 'because of this fear. I'm not afraid of danger. What frightens me is fear itself. At the moment I am fighting against fear, but sooner or later I won't be able to fight any more.'

During long conversations with Usher I learnt more about his strange illness. He was sure that it came from the House of Usher itself. He had not left the house for many years and he had become, he thought, as sad as the house itself. The gloom of its grey walls and its dark silent lake had become his own.

He also believed that much of his sadness was because his dear sister was seriously ill. He had one sister, Madeleine, the only other person in his family who was still living, but each day she seemed a little nearer to death.

'Her death,' Usher said blackly, 'will leave me alone in the world, the last of all the Ushers.'

While he was speaking, Madeleine passed slowly through the back of the long room and, without noticing me, disappeared. As I looked at her, my eyes felt heavy with sleep, and I had a strange feeling of fear. I looked across at Usher. He had covered his face with his hands, but I could see that he had become even paler, and that he was crying silently.

Lady Madeleine's illness was a mysterious one which no doctor could understand. Every day she became weaker and thinner, and sometimes went into a sleep which was more like death than sleep. For years she had fought bravely against her illness, but on the night of my arrival she went to bed and did not get up from it again. 'You will probably not see her again alive,' Usher said to me, shaking his head sadly.

During the next few days Usher and I never spoke about

his sister. We spent a lot of time painting and reading together, and sometimes he played on his guitar. I tried very hard to help my friend, but I realized that his sadness was too deep. It was a black gloom that covered everything that belonged to his world; sometimes, indeed, he seemed close to the edge of madness.

He painted strange pictures, and sang mysterious songs with wild words. His ideas, too, were strange, and he had one idea that seemed more important to him than all the others. He was quite sure that all things, plants, trees, even stones, were able to *feel*.

'The House of Usher itself,' he told me, 'is like a living thing. When the walls were first built, life went into the stones themselves and year after year it has grown stronger. Even the air around the walls and above the lake has its own life, and belongs to the house. Don't you see,' he cried, 'how the stones and the air have shaped the lives of the Usher family?'

These ideas were too fantastic for me, and I could not answer him.

One evening I was reading quietly when my friend told me, in very few words, that the Lady Madeleine had died. He had decided, he said, to keep her body for a fortnight in one of the vaults under the house, before it went to its last resting-place. This was because his sister's illness had been a mysterious one, and her doctors wanted to learn more about it. He asked me to help him and I agreed.

Together we carried the body in its coffin down to the vaults under the house. The vault that he had chosen was a long way down, but was under the part of the house where

Together we carried the body in its coffin down to the vaults.

I slept. It had once been a prison, and was small, dark, and airless, with a heavy metal door.

We put the coffin down and then gently lifted up the cover to look at the dead woman for the last time. As I looked down at her face, I realized how much Usher's sister looked like him. My friend then said a few quiet words and I learnt that he and his sister had been born on the same day. Each had known the other's mind without the need for words.

We could not look at her for long. Her strange illness had left her with a soft pink colour on her face, and that unchanging half-smile on her lips which is so terrible in death. We put back the cover of the coffin, fixed it down well, and after locking the heavy door of the vault, went back upstairs into the gloomy house.

After some days of deep unhappiness, I saw that my friend's illness of the mind was growing worse. He did not paint or read any more. He moved slowly from room to room, never knowing what to do. His face became paler, the light disappeared from his eyes, and his voice often shook with fear when he spoke. Sometimes I thought he was trying to tell me some terrible secret. At other times I thought he was going mad. He used to sit for hours, looking at nothing, listening to nothing – except the sounds in his own mind. I myself began to know real fear. I felt my friend's terror, his deep gloom, slowly taking hold of my own mind.

About seven or eight days after we had put Lady Madeleine's coffin in the vault, I went to bed but could not sleep. Hour after hour I lay there, fighting the fear and gloom that filled my mind. Outside, there was a storm which was growing wilder, and my room was full of shadows and the dark shapes of the gloomy furniture. I tried to calm myself, but I only became more frightened.

Suddenly, my body shook with a new terror. I sat up in bed and listened hard. Yes, I could hear some low sounds, coming not from the storm outside, but from somewhere inside the house. Quickly, I put on my clothes and started walking up and down the room, trying to shake off my terrible fear.

Then I heard a knock on my door and Usher came in. His face was as white as it had always been, and there was a kind of madness in his eyes. The look on his face frightened me terribly, but at the same time I was pleased not to be alone any more.

For some moments he looked around without saying a word. Then, suddenly, 'Have you not seen it? No? Then wait. You must see it.' He hurried to the window and opened it.

The wind from the violent storm outside crashed into the room, nearly knocking us to the floor. It was, indeed, a wild, but strangely beautiful night. The wind seemed to be going in circles around the house, and huge, heavy black clouds chased each other, first this way, then that way. We could see no moon and no stars, but a pale ghostly light lay around the house.

'You mustn't, no, you must not watch this,' I cried to Usher. I pushed him gently away from the window and to a seat. 'It's only a storm, and the cold night air will be dangerous to your health. Let's close the window and read together. Look, here's one of your favourite books. I will read to you, and you can listen, and so we will pass this terrible night together.'

It was a wild, but strangely beautiful night.

The book which I had picked up was *The Sad, Mad Life* of Sir Launcelot Canning. It was not really one of Usher's favourite books, but it was the only one that I had near me, so I started to read it. It was a wild, fantastic story, but I hoped that my reading would make Usher calmer and less afraid. He listened to me, indeed, but with a kind of mad seriousness that I found frightening.

I read for a while and reached the place in the book where Ethelred broke down the door of the old man's house.

Now Ethelred decided he could wait outside in the storm no longer. He lifted his heavy stick and beat against the wooden door until he had made a hole. Then with his hands he pulled the door to pieces. The noise of the dry wood cracking and breaking could be heard all through the forest.

As I finished reading this sentence, I jumped in my seat and then sat very still. I thought that I had heard, from somewhere far away in the house, the same noise of cracking and breaking wood. But I could not hear it clearly, and the noise of the storm was much louder. I continued reading:

Ethelred entered the house but could not see the old man. Then the house disappeared and he saw a dragon, with fire coming out of its mouth. Ethelred lifted his heavy stick and brought it crashing down on the dragon's head. As the dragon fell dying to the ground, it gave a terrible cry – a long, hard, unnatural scream.

Here again I stopped suddenly. I was sure that I could

hear a cry. It was low and far away, but it was a long screaming sound – just like the one described in the book.

Although I was feeling so nervous, I tried hard to hide my terror. I was not sure if Usher had heard the sounds that I had heard. In the last few minutes he had moved and was now sitting with his face towards the door. But I could see that his lips were shaking and his body was moving gently from side to side. I continued reading the story:

And now Ethelred, after he had killed the dragon, turned and saw in front of him a palace of gold with tall gates of shining silver in the walls. Bravely, Ethelred ran towards the palace, but the shining silver gates did not wait for his coming and fell to the ground at his feet with a great and terrible ringing sound.

As I read these words, I heard clearly the loud, heavy sound of metal falling. I jumped to my feet, but Usher sat in his seat and did not move. I ran towards him. He was looking straight in front of him and his face was like stone. As I placed my hand on his arm, his body began to shake. A sickly smile came over his lips, and he spoke in a low hurried voice. He did not seem to realize that I was there. I put my head close to his to catch his words.

'Don't I hear it? – yes, I hear it, and I *have* heard it. For many minutes, many hours, many days I have heard it – but I was too frightened, too frightened to speak. *We have put her alive into her coffin!* Did I not tell you that I could hear even the softest sound? I tell you now that I heard her move in the coffin. I heard the sounds many days ago, but my terror was too great – *I could not speak!* And now tonight

'*WE HAVE PUT HER ALIVE INTO HER COFFIN!*'

– when you read about Ethelred breaking the old man's door, about the cry of the dragon, and the falling of the gates – it was, in fact, the breaking of her coffin, the scream of metal as she broke open the vault, and the ringing crash as the metal door fell to the floor! Oh, where can I escape to? Is she hurrying towards me at this very minute? Is that her angry footstep that I can hear on the stairs? Can I hear the heavy and terrible beating of her heart? MADMAN!'

He jumped up and shouted, screaming out his words like a man dying in terror. 'MADMAN! I TELL YOU THAT AT THIS MINUTE SHE IS STANDING OUTSIDE THIS DOOR!'

As he screamed these words, the heavy door was thrown open by the strong wind. There, outside the door, dressed in the white clothes of the dead, stood the tall figure of the Lady Madeleine of Usher. There was blood on her hands, her arms, her torn white clothes. Every part of her body showed the marks of her long fight to escape from the coffin. For a moment she stood there shaking, moving slowly from side to side. Then with a low cry she fell heavily onto her brother. And in the moment of her now final death, he fell with her to the floor – a dead man, killed by his own terror.

From that room, and from that house, I ran in horror. Outside, the storm was still violent and as I ran past the lake, a sudden wild light shone around me. I turned to see where this strange light was coming from. It was the moon, a full, blood-red moon, shining through a narrow crack in the walls of the house. It was the crack which started at the roof of the building and went right down to the ground. As I watched, the crack grew larger, the wind grew wilder

It was the moon, a full, blood-red moon,
shining through a crack in the walls.

– now I could see the full circle of the blood-red moon, and the great walls of the house breaking and falling. There was a long shouting sound, like the voice of a thousand waters, and the deep dark lake closed over the broken pieces of the House of Usher.

The Black Cat

I know you will not believe this story. Only a madman could hope that you would believe it – and I am not mad. But as I am going to die tomorrow, I would like to tell my story to the world today. Perhaps some day, somebody more calm and less excitable than me, will be able to explain it.

I have always loved animals. I loved them deeply, from the very first days of my life. When I was young, we always had many animals in our house, and so I used to spend most of my days playing with them and taking care of them. As the years passed, I grew into a quiet, gentle man, and my love for animals grew too. I found that they were more friendly, more honest than most men. Animals were always my best friends.

I got married when I was quite young. Luckily, my wife loved animals too, and she used to buy me many animals as presents. In fact, our house was always full of animals – we had birds, fish, a dog, chickens, and *a cat*.

This cat, whom we called Pluto, was a large black cat. He was a beautiful animal, and he was also very clever. I loved Pluto more than I loved all my other animals. I wanted to do everything for him myself, so I never let my wife take care of him. I used to play with him and give him his food, and he followed me everywhere I went.

For several years Pluto and I were the best of friends, but during this time my life slowly changed. I became a heavy drinker, and my need for alcohol soon grew into a terrible

Our house was always full of animals.

disease. I was often angry and violent. I began to shout at my wife, and I even started to hit her. My animals, too, felt the change in me. I stopped taking care of them and sometimes I was even cruel to them. But I was never cruel to Pluto. As time passed, my disease grew worse, and soon even Pluto was not safe from my violence.

One night I arrived home late. I was very, very drunk. When Pluto saw me, he tried to run away from me, and this made me angry. I caught him by his neck and shook him. He, in his fright, bit me on the hand. At once, a wild, terrible anger filled me, and I could feel nothing except burning hate. Slowly I took a knife from my pocket, opened it, and then carefully cut out one of Pluto's eyes from its socket. I shake today as I write these words down. Every time I remember that day, I still feel sadness and pain.

When I woke up the next morning, I felt ashamed of what I had done. But this feeling was not strong enough to make me change my life. I continued to drink because it was too difficult for me to stop. Soon, I had forgotten what I had done.

As the months passed, Pluto got better. His empty eye socket still looked terrible, but at least he wasn't in pain any more. Not surprisingly, he used to run away from me when he saw me, frightened that I would hurt him again. At first I was sad to see him run away – an animal which had once so loved me. Then I began to feel a little angry. There is something strange about the human heart. We humans seem to like hurting ourselves. Haven't we all, a hundred times, done something stupid or evil just because we know that we should not do it? It was because of this, this need to hurt myself, that I did this next evil thing . . .

One morning I woke, found a rope and calmly tied it round Pluto's neck. Then I hung the poor animal from a tree and left it there to die. I cried as I did this terrible thing. My face was wet with tears and my heart was black and heavy. But I killed it. I killed it *because* I knew it had loved me, *because* it hadn't hurt me, even *because* I knew that I was doing something terrible and wrong.

That same night we had a fire in our house. I was woken from my sleep by loud shouts of 'Fire!' When I opened my eyes, I found that the fire had already reached the bedroom. My wife and I ran out of the house as fast as we could. Luckily

I hung the poor animal from a tree and left it there to die.

we escaped death, but the house and almost everything in it was destroyed.

The next day I went back into the house and saw several people standing in a group, looking at a wall. It was the only wall of the house that was still standing after the fire. It was one of my bedroom walls, the one where the head of my bed had rested. As I came nearer to the wall I heard someone say, 'How strange!' and another person, 'That's impossible!' And then I saw it – a huge cat. Not a real cat, but the shape of a cat outlined in the white bedroom wall. It was as clear as a picture. I could even see a rope around the animal's neck.

I stood there in horror, too frightened to move. Then, slowly, I thought back to the night before. I had left the cat hanging from a tree, in the garden at the back of my house. When a neighbour had first noticed the fire, many people had run into the garden. One of them had probably cut the cat from the tree and thrown it through my open window, in order to wake me up. The cat's body had hit my bedroom wall and left its shape there, because the plaster on that wall was new and still soft.

Although I thought that this was a very reasonable explanation, the strange shape on the wall still worried me. I thought about the cat day and night. I began to feel sorry that I had killed it. I started walking around the streets at night looking at all the cats, to see if I could find another one like Pluto.

One night, I was drinking in my favourite bar when I suddenly noticed a large, black cat. I went up to it and touched it. It was very large – as large as Pluto had been. It also looked very like Pluto. Except for one thing. Pluto had been black all over, but this cat had a white mark on its front.

I touched the cat and he immediately lay down against my leg and seemed very friendly towards me. This, I decided, was the cat that I wanted. I offered the barman some money to buy the cat from him, but he said that the cat didn't belong to him. In fact, he had no idea where it had come from.

So I took the cat home. My wife liked it immediately, and it stayed with us from that day. But soon – I do not know why – the cat started to make me angry, and, as time passed, I began to hate it. I did not hurt it in any way, but I always tried to keep as far away from it as possible.

I knew one reason why I hated this cat so much. On the morning after I had brought it home, I saw that, like Pluto, it had lost one of its eyes. My wife, who was the kind, gentle person that I had once been, only loved the cat more because of this. But the cat didn't like my wife. It loved me alone.

Every time I sat down, it used to jump onto my knees. When I went out of a room, it used to run out in front of me and get between my feet, or climb up my legs. At these times, I wanted to kill it. But I didn't, because I was too afraid – afraid of the cat, and even more afraid of the white mark on its chest.

I have already mentioned this mark. At first, there was nothing strange about it. It was just a white mark. But slowly this mark grew and changed until it had the clear shape of a terrible, a horrible thing – I find it difficult, here in my prison, to write the word. It was the shape of the GALLOWS! Yes, those horrible wooden posts from which they hang men by a rope around the neck!

'*It was the shape of the* GALLOWS!'

As each day passed, my fear grew and grew. I, a man, a strong man, had become afraid of a cat! Why was I so frightened, so worried by a stupid animal? Day and night, I could get no rest. I had the most terrible dreams, and my mind turned to dark, evil thoughts. I hated everything, everybody – and life itself.

One day my wife and I needed to get something from the cellar underneath the house. The cat followed us down the steps and threw itself in front of me. I almost fell on my face and, mad with anger, I took hold of an axe and tried to kill the animal. But my wife caught my arm to stop me, and then anger exploded in my mind. I turned and drove the axe deep into her head. She fell dead on the floor, without a sound.

After this horrible murder, I calmly made plans to hide the body. I knew I couldn't take it out of the house, either by day or night, because the neighbours would see me. So I had to think of other ways . . . I could cut the body up into very small pieces and then burn them in a fire. I could hide the body under the floor. Or I could put the body in a box and then ask someone to carry the box away . . . Finally, I thought of a better idea. I decided to hide the body behind the walls of the cellar.

I knew immediately which wall to choose. There was a wall in the cellar round the bottom of an old chimney, which was no longer used. This wall had bricks in the front and back but was empty in the middle. I started work at once. I took out some of the bricks from the front wall and carefully put the body against the back wall. Then I put back the bricks and covered them with plaster. I made sure that the plaster did not look new, and soon the wall looked just the same as all the other walls. When I had finished my work, I looked at the plaster. 'I've never done a better piece of work!' I said to myself happily.

I then looked around for the cat, to kill it. It had brought too much unhappiness into my life, and so it, too, must now

Anger exploded in my mind.

die. I looked for it everywhere, but it had disappeared. I was free at last! That night I had a deep, peaceful sleep – I, who had just killed my wife, slept well!

Three days passed and still the cat did not appear. I was now a happy man, happier than I had been for a long time. I wasn't worried by what I had done. People had asked a few questions and the police had visited my house, but they had found nothing.

On the fourth day the police visited again and began to search the house. They looked into all the rooms and then went down into the cellar. I went with them, feeling calm and safe. I watched them as they looked everywhere. They seemed quite happy that there was nothing there and they got ready to leave. I was very happy. I was sure that I was safe, but I wanted to say something, just a word or two, to show how unworried I was.

'Gentlemen,' I said, 'I'm pleased that you've found nothing here, and that you are now leaving this house . . . But let me show you something, gentlemen. Do you see how well built this house is? These walls, you will notice, are very strong.' As I said these words, I knocked on the wall with a stick – the wall where I had hidden my wife!

At that moment we heard a sound. It was a strange sound, unlike anything I had ever heard before. The sound was soft at first, almost like a baby crying. Then it grew louder and louder and turned into one long, endless scream. It was like a cry rising from Hell.

The policemen looked at me, then at one another. They ran to the wall and started pulling out the bricks as fast as they could. In minutes the wall was down and there, for all to see, was the body of my dead wife. On top of her head, with a red, open mouth and one burning eye, sat the black cat – the animal which had made me a murderer, and which would now send me to my death.

I had put the horrible thing into the wall, alive, with my wife!

The Masque of the Red Death

The Red Death had been in the country for many, many years. No disease had ever been so deadly. People called it the Red Death because it left blood, red horrible blood, on the body and face of each person it visited. And no one, if visited, was ever left alive. Once a person was touched by the Red Death, he immediately felt pains, and soon afterwards started to bleed from every part of his body. In thirty minutes he was dead. After that no one, not even his family, went near the blood-covered body.

Everybody was afraid of the Red Death – everybody except the fearless Prince Prospero. *He* refused to be troubled by it. Although half the people of his country had already died from this terrible disease, he continued to enjoy life to the full. One day he decided to invite a thousand of his strong and brave friends to stay with him in one of his castles, far out in the countryside. There the Red Death would not be able to touch them.

It was a huge and extraordinary castle, built to Prince Prospero's own plan. It had strong high walls and great gates of heavy metal. Now when the Prince and his friends arrived at the castle gates they went inside, locked the gates carefully and threw away the keys. In that way no one would be able to enter or escape. They were all there together, far away from the Red Death. Now they could forget the world outside and think only of themselves. They had everything they needed to amuse themselves, because the Prince had forgotten

Outside the castle lay the Red Death.

nothing. He had brought in food and wine, actors, musicians, and dancers. All of this, and life itself, was inside the castle. Outside lay the Red Death.

Towards the end of the fifth or sixth month, while the Red Death was at its most deadly outside, the Prince gave a wonderful masked ball for his friends. It was a wild and wonderful ball, but first let me tell you about the rooms in which he gave the ball. There were seven rooms in all. In most castles, of course, the rooms for great parties or dances join each other end to end. In this way, when the doors at the end of each room are opened, the seven rooms become one huge room, and you can see from the first room right through to the last one. In Prospero's castle, it was different. Each room turned suddenly round a corner into the next, so if you were standing in one room it was impossible to see into the other rooms.

In the middle of each wall, on the right and left, there was a tall, narrow window opening onto the closed passage which ran along beside all seven rooms. Each window was made of different coloured glass, and the colour of the glass was the same as the colour of the room that it opened onto. The first room, for example, was blue, and so its windows were also a deep blue. The second room was purple, and so the windows, too, were purple. The third was green, with green windows, the fourth orange, the fifth white, and the sixth violet. The seventh room was black. Its walls were black, its thick, heavy carpet was also black. But its windows were red – a deep blood-red.

There were no candles in any of the rooms. The only light came from fires, in hanging metal baskets, which were in the passages outside the rooms. Each fire was opposite a window, and so the light from the fire shone through the coloured glass and filled each room with strange and fantastic shadows. But in the black room the firelight that shone through the blood-red window changed the room into something too horrible to describe. In that strange light, faces became wild and frightening, and few people were brave enough to enter the room at all.

In this room, against the farthest wall, stood a huge black clock. Every hour it chimed loud and deep and clear, filling the castle with its long, gloomy sound. And while the clock chimed, the musicians stopped playing and even the wildest dancers stood still, in silence and fear, listening to the passing of another hour . . . But when the chiming stopped, people looked at each other and laughed, trying hard to pretend that they had not been frightened. Happiness came into the castle again, until the clock chimed the passing of the next hour, and the same fear returned.

Prince Prospero's ball, although given in these strange rooms, was wild and happy. The Prince had planned everything – the colours, the paintings on the walls, even the cloaks and masks worn by each one of his friends. He had chosen all the clothes with the greatest of care, putting together the beautiful and the ugly, the strange and the fantastic, the surprising and the frightening.

Each man and woman was dressed like a terrible dream. And in and out of the rooms these dreams walked and danced, their clothes changing colour each time they entered a different room. But no one was brave enough now to enter the black room. As the night passed and the fires burned brighter, the colours and shapes in this room became more horrible than ever. The black carpet and walls seemed full of gloom, and the deep chimes of the black clock sounded even more frightening.

But the other six rooms were full of life and pleasure. People were dancing and singing, talking and laughing, and the wild noise of a thousand happy men and women rang through the castle. Then came the hour of midnight, and once again dancers and musicians became still and silent, as the clock slowly rang the twelve long chimes of midnight. And because the twelve chimes took a long time to ring, each person had more time to think, and feel

Each man and woman was dressed like a terrible dream.

uncomfortable. They also had time, before the last chime had sounded, to notice a masked figure who had not been there before. The first person who saw the stranger told the next person, who told another, and in a few minutes a cry of fear and horror rose up from the crowd.

Now you will remember that everyone at the ball was wearing strange cloaks and masks, which belonged more to the world of dreams and wild imagination than to everyday life. So why, you may ask, this horror, and this fear? But

even in the cruellest heart there are some fears too terrible
to laugh at. The tall thin figure of the stranger was dressed
from head to foot in the white clothes of the dead. And the
mask over the face was frighteningly real – it was the face
of a dead man. Worse still, the face and the body were covered
with red, horrible blood! Here, in the middle of all that
dancing and happiness was a living picture of the Red Death!

When Prince Prospero saw the masked stranger, his face
became white with fear. Then his fear turned to anger and
he shouted out, 'Who is that? Who is mad enough to play
games with us, and with death, in this way? Take hold of
him, and pull off his mask. I want to see the face of the man
who, tomorrow, will hang from the castle roof.'

The Prince was in the blue room as he said these words.
They rang loudly and clearly through the seven rooms. Many
of the Prince's friends started to run towards the masked
figure, but they were all too frightened to touch him. With
slow and silent steps, the stranger walked slowly towards
the Prince, passing very near to him. Then he continued
walking, and went from the blue room into the purple one,
from the purple into the green, and then into the orange
room, the white room and then the violet room. No one
tried to stop him.

Then Prince Prospero, mad with anger, hurried through
the six rooms, with a sword in his hand. As the masked figure
entered the black room, the Prince was close behind him,
holding his sword up high. At that moment the stranger
turned suddenly to look at the Prince. There was a loud cry
– and the sword fell upon the black carpet, followed by the
dead body of the fearless Prince Prospero.

He was standing very still, in the shadow of the black clock.

At once a crowd of people ran into the black room and took hold of the masked stranger. He was standing very still, in the shadow of the black clock. Angrily, they pulled away the clothes and the mask, but then they backed away in horror, because inside the clothes and mask they found – nothing.

And now each person in the castle understood that the Red Death was there, among them. It had come like a thief in the night. And one by one they fell down dead. And the black clock stopped ringing with the death of the last person. And the fires also died away. And the only things left in the castle were Darkness and the Red Death.

William Wilson

William Wilson is not my name. But I shall use it in this story because my real name is too well known, too hated in every corner of the world. My evil crimes have made sure of that. And as the day of my death comes nearer, I feel the need to write, to explain to you how my life of crime began.

Most men become evil slowly. They start with little crimes and then move on to bigger ones. But I am different. I moved into real crime with just one big step. Has any man lived a life as evil as mine? But now, the shadow of death fills me with fear; day and night I have the most terrible dreams. Perhaps someone, somewhere, will feel sorry for me. Listen to my story . . .

I was a wild and excitable child. My parents worried about me and often tried to punish me, but they never succeeded in changing me. I refused to obey them and I never followed any orders that they gave me. I wanted to be free so I listened only to myself.

The first school that I can remember was a large and very old house in a small, quiet English village. As I write, I can still feel the coolness of the shadowy gardens near the house. I can smell the sweetness of the flowers and hear the deep sound of the church bells as they rang every hour.

These feelings give me some moments of happiness as I sit here in black misery, waiting for death. In fact, it is here, in this school, that my story really begins . . .

The school building was large and old. The big gardens

were closed in by a high wall, with broken glass at the top, just like a prison. We only went out three times a week. On Saturday afternoons we took a walk in some fields near the school, under the watchful eye of one of our teachers. On Sundays we went out twice, morning and evening, to go to the village church.

I was not bored or unhappy during my life at school. Children can amuse themselves very easily, and in my imagination, I lived an exciting life, full of mystery and interest. But in the real world, the days were always the same – we woke up and went to bed, we walked in the fields and played in the playground . . . The playground was, indeed, a very special place. It was a place where friends were made and lost, a place always full of trouble and excitement.

I was the kind of boy who liked to give orders, not to take them. I always wanted to win every game, every fight, and to be first in everything. All the other boys, even those a bit older than myself, were happy to follow and obey me. All, that is, except one. His name was the same as mine, so I shall call him William Wilson, too. We were not from the same family, but we both had the same name. This was not surprising because my name was not an unusual one.

This William Wilson refused to obey me. He argued with me, both in class and in the playground, and tried to stop the other boys from following me. Actually, I think I was the only boy who realized what he was doing. He did everything very cleverly and silently, and in this way nobody really noticed it. But I – I noticed what he did, and I was frightened by it. I was afraid that Wilson was stronger than I was. I became worried and angry when I saw the other

He argued with me, both in class and in the playground.

boys follow him instead of me. But Wilson was always cool and calm. Nothing ever troubled him. He seemed to want one thing only – to see me frightened and unhappy. But at the same time I sometimes noticed that he showed a friendliness towards me – which was most unwelcome to me.

It is difficult for me to describe my feelings towards Wilson. I didn't hate him, but neither did I like him. I think that, more than anything, I felt afraid of him. At the same time I wanted to know more about him. I wanted to find something that frightened or worried him. But I could find nothing. There was nothing strange in the way he looked or walked. Nothing, that is, except for one thing – his voice. His voice was strange. When he spoke, he could never speak loudly. In fact, he never spoke above a whisper.

Wilson was quick to find the one thing that I really did not like. It was my name. Although I come from an old and famous family, my name is a very everyday one. It could belong to any unimportant workman. I had always hated my name, but now I hated it even more because both of us had the same name. I heard it twice as often. And there was something that worried me even more deeply. We seemed to look alike as well. We were as tall as one another, we were both thin, and even our faces were alike. Because our names were the same, I knew that the older boys thought that we were brothers, but nobody seemed to notice that we looked alike. But Wilson noticed it and he also saw that I was angry about it. Nothing ever escaped him. He always knew my deepest feelings.

After a while he started to dress like me, and even to walk

like me. Luckily, he could not speak like me when I spoke loudly, but when I spoke in a whisper, *his whisper was just like mine.*

All these things troubled me deeply. I could see that Wilson enjoyed making me angry, and he used to laugh at me secretly. Strangely, the other boys never noticed how he made fun of me, and copied me in every way. I was the only one who noticed it.

Very often he used to give me advice, telling me quietly what I should do or what I should say. I hated him even more when he did this. Today, of course, I realize that his advice was always very good and sensible. What a pity that I never followed it!

As time went by, I became more and more angry with him. Why should he, or anyone, give *me* advice? My feelings towards him changed and I actually began to hate him. He noticed this and tried not to come near me so much.

One day, towards the end of my fifth year at school we had a violent argument. While we were arguing, he showed his feelings more openly than usual, and a very strange idea came into my mind. I thought – how can I describe it? – I thought just for a second or two that I had known him before, a long, long time ago, when we were very young children. It was, as I say, a strange and very stupid idea, and I forgot it as quickly as I could.

But that night, when everyone was asleep, I got out of bed. Then I walked through the dark building, with a small lantern in my hands, until I reached Wilson's room. I left the lantern outside and went near to his bed. Yes, he was asleep. I returned to get my lantern and went back to his bed. I had planned to do something cruel to him while he slept. But as I looked at the sleeping boy, my heart beat faster and I was filled with fear. Was this really what William Wilson looked like? Did he look just the same when he was awake? I knew that he was as tall as I was. I knew, too, that he walked like me and talked like me, and copied me in every way that he could. But was it possible that the person in that bed looked so like me in every way? I began to shake with fear, and my body turned ice-cold. Surely he couldn't look like this! Was I really looking at a boy who was not just a copy of me, but . . .

I was more frightened than I had ever been in my life. I went silently out of his room, left the school building and never returned there again.

After several lazy months at home, I was sent to Eton, one of the most famous English boys' schools. There, I soon forgot William Wilson and the strange fears I had felt. If I thought about them at all, I used to laugh at myself.

My life at Eton lasted for three wild and evil years. I learnt to be clever and secret, and was interested only in new ways of amusing myself. I chose the worst kind of students for my friends, and spent all my time in evil enjoyment. One night, when I was in my third year, I invited some students to a party in my rooms. We drank and played cards all through the night. As well as the wine, we had other, perhaps more dangerous, pleasures. As the first morning light started to appear, I suggested a new evil amusement. Then I noticed that somebody was opening my door and I heard a servant's voice, 'There's somebody outside who wants to speak to you, sir. He seems to be in a hurry.'

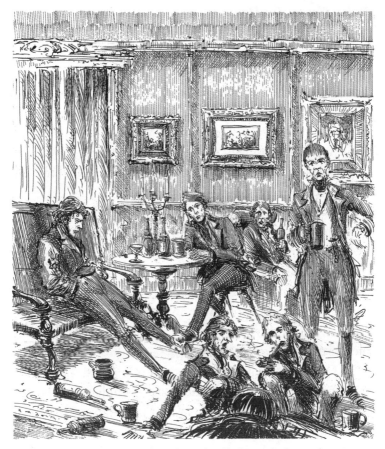

We drank and played cards all through the night.

I walked, with difficulty, to the hall, as I was feeling very drunk with the wine. It was still too dark to see clearly, but I could just see the shape of a young man. He was as tall as I was, and was wearing the same clothes as myself. I could not see his face.

He came up to me and whispered the words 'William

Wilson!' in my ear. I knew the voice at once. It was impossible to mistake it. Those two words were enough to fill me with fear. Before I could look into his face, he had disappeared.

The meeting only lasted a few seconds, but for some weeks I could not forget it. I thought of it all the time. Who and what was this William Wilson? Where did he come from? What did he want from me? My questions stayed unanswered, but I did discover one thing. I learnt that William Wilson had left my last school on the same day that I myself had run away from it.

Soon I forgot about him again, and not long afterwards I went up to Oxford University. My parents were not sensible people and they always gave me a lot of money. I was able to live a fashionable, expensive life, and to choose as my friends the sons of the richest families of England. There was nothing at all to stop me now. I spent my money wildly, and passed my days and nights in dangerous and exciting pleasures.

At Oxford I spent a lot of my time gambling. I became, in fact, a most clever and successful gambler – no better than a thief. I played cards in order to win money from the other students and become even richer. Of course, I was careful to play only with students who were bad at playing cards. In this way I could be sure of winning every time. My friends were not clever enough to see what I was doing.

In my second year at University I met a new student called Glendinning. He came from an old English family and was one of the richest students in the university. I soon realized that he was very unintelligent and because of this he was, of course, a very suitable person for me to gamble with! I started to play cards with him often, and for some time I made sure that he always won.

At last I decided that the time was right and I made my plans carefully. I met Glendinning at the rooms of a friend of mine, a Mr Preston (who had no idea of my secret plan). Eight or ten other friends were also invited. In this way Glendinning had no idea that I planned to gamble with him that evening. In fact, at the party, it was he who first suggested playing cards.

We played for many long hours. In the end, by my careful plan, I was playing alone against Glendinning, while the others watched our game. Glendinning had drunk a lot of wine during the evening and his hands were beginning to shake a little – from fear or from the wine, I wasn't sure. He had already lost a large amount of money. Then he did what I had hoped for. He took another long drink of wine and said, 'Let's double the stakes.' Beginners always think they can win back what they have lost in this way.

At first I pretended to refuse. Then he became angry, so, naturally, I had to agree. My plan was working excellently. We continued playing, and in less than an hour my winnings were four times as big. Glendinning's face was now as white as a sheet. Everyone around the table started talking, and to my surprise I heard the words, 'That's the end of Glendinning. He's just lost everything he had!'

I had heard that Glendinning was very rich indeed – rich enough to lose a lot of money and not to worry about it. Now, I understood from the whispers around the table, that this was not true. I had, in fact, won everything he owned, and so destroyed him.

Nobody spoke. Glendinning had covered his face with his hands and everyone clearly felt very sorry for him. Even I began to feel a little worried, and wondered what I should do.

As we stood in silence, the doors suddenly opened and a strong wind filled the room. It blew out all the candles in the room and we were left in darkness. But in the few seconds before the candles went out, we noticed that a man had entered the room. He was about as tall as I was, and his face and body were hidden by a long cloak. As we stood in the darkness, we could *feel* him standing in the room.

Then he began to speak. He spoke in a whisper, and his voice filled me with fear. 'Gentlemen,' he said. 'I am here because I have something important to tell you. I am afraid that you do not really know the man who has just won so much money from Glendinning. Let me tell you how to learn more about him. Please look very carefully inside his left sleeve and at the several little packets inside the large pockets of his jacket.' Immediately after these words he left the room, as silently as he had entered it.

That moment was one of the worst moments of my life. I had no time to do anything. My friends fell on me angrily, lit the candles again, and searched my clothes. They found the single cards hidden carefully inside my left sleeve, and in my pockets they discovered the packets of special cards which helped me to win every game I played.

My friends stood around me in a circle and looked at me in silence. Mr Preston then picked up a cloak from the floor. 'Mr Wilson,' he said. 'Here is your cloak. You will, I hope, leave my room, and then leave Oxford immediately.'

My friends fell on me angrily, and searched my clothes.

I wanted to hit him, but something stopped me. It was the cloak that Preston was holding in his hands. Although it looked like my cloak, I knew that it wasn't, because my own cloak was already over my left arm. It was a very unusual and expensive cloak, which a shop had made specially for me. How was it possible that there was now another cloak just like it?

I thought back to the moment when the stranger had come into the room. Yes, *he* had been wearing a cloak too . . . Full of fear, I quickly took the cloak from Mr Preston and left the room. The next morning I left Oxford and escaped to Europe. I was now known to be a cheat at cards and every door in England would be closed against me.

But bad luck travelled with me. In fact I soon realized that my troubles at Oxford had been only the beginning . . . Soon after I arrived in Paris, I met William Wilson again. There, too, he destroyed my evil hopes. Everywhere I went, year after year, he appeared like a ghost and came between me and my plans. In Rome he stopped me from getting what I wanted. In Vienna, too – in Berlin, and even in Moscow! Wasn't there anywhere where I could be left alone? I went from city to city, trying to escape from him. But I couldn't feel free. I couldn't be alone. He followed me everywhere.

Again and again I used to ask myself these questions. 'Who is he? Where does he come from? What does he want from me?' But I could find no answer. I thought deeply about all the times when I had seen him. In every city, I realized, Wilson had done the same thing. He had not stopped my plans all the time, but only when they were evil and dangerous, either to others or to myself. I understood all this, but still I was

*Everywhere I went, year after year, he appeared like
a ghost and came between me and my plans.*

very angry. Why couldn't Wilson leave me alone? Why couldn't he let me live in the way I wanted to?

I realized another thing too. Every time Wilson appeared, he had never let me see his face. I had always noticed his clothes. It was difficult not to notice them because they were always the same as mine. But he kept his face hidden from me. Why did he do this? Did he really think that I was so stupid? Did he think I hadn't realized who he was? The man who followed me everywhere and destroyed my plans again and again was the same William Wilson of my schooldays! But let me continue with my story.

Until now I had felt afraid of Wilson and had obeyed him. The mystery of his sudden arrivals, his cleverness, his deep understanding of me – all these things filled me with fear. I always obeyed him, although I hated myself for doing it. But recently I had become a very heavy drinker. Wine made me feel brave and strong, able to fight anybody who tried to stop me. At the same time I began to think that Wilson was becoming weaker. Was this really happening or was it just a dream? I cannot tell, but I do know that my own feelings were becoming more and more violent. I began to feel a burning hope – soon I would break free from this terrible enemy and never take his orders again.

One evening, in 18—, I was in Rome and was invited to a big party in the palace of Duke Di Broglio. The Duke was old and boring, but his wife was young and beautiful, and not very sensible. I had evil plans for her. She and I had agreed to meet, during the party, in a quiet room where we could be alone.

As I walked from room to room looking for her in the

crowds, I suddenly felt a hand touch my arm. Then I heard a *whisper* in my ears. Angrily I turned round and saw a man. He was wearing the same clothes as I was, but his face was covered with a black mask. I caught him by his arm. 'Stop!' I shouted. 'I have had enough trouble from you! This is the last time you'll follow me anywhere! Come with me now

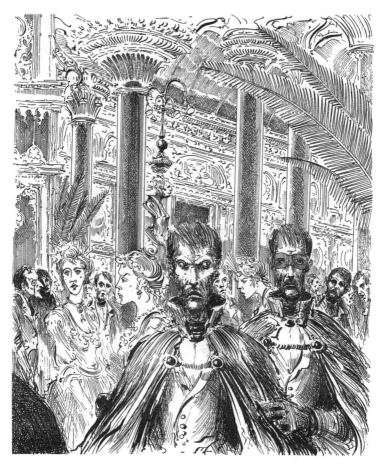

His face was covered with a black mask.

into the next room. If you don't, I shall kill you right now, here where you stand!'

I took him into a small room nearby and pushed him violently to the floor. He got to his feet shakily, and stood up against the wall. I then closed the door and ordered him to fight. For a second he did not move. Then he silently took out his sword.

It was a short fight. I was wild and excited and felt stronger than I had ever felt before. After only a few seconds I pushed him against the wall and plunged my sword into his body again and again.

At that moment somebody tried to open the door. I ran to check that the door was locked and then ran back towards my enemy. How can I describe what I saw at that moment? During those few seconds when I had turned to the door, the room had become strangely different. There was now a large mirror at the end of the room. I was sure that it had not been there before. As I stepped up to the mirror, I saw myself, walking forward shakily, my face white and covered with blood.

Or so I thought. But I was wrong. It was my enemy, Wilson, who stood before me in his last moments of life. His mask and cloak lay on the floor. His face was now uncovered. And I saw, in terror, that his face was *my own*!

Then Wilson spoke, but no longer in a whisper, and I thought I heard my own voice speaking as he said:

'You have won, and I have lost. But from this moment you, too, are dead – dead to the world, to Heaven, and to hope! You lived in me – and, in my death, look in my face, which is your own, and see how you have murdered yourself.'

The Tell-Tale Heart

It is true that I had been – and I am – very nervous, but do you really think that I am mad? I could see and hear *more* clearly – not less, because of the disease. My hearing, more than anything, was excellent. I could hear all things, things in this world and things in heaven. I heard many things in hell, too. So how can I be mad? See how clearly and calmly I can tell my story.

I cannot explain how the idea first came into my head. But once I had thought of the idea, I could not forget it. I had no reason to do it. I was not angry. I loved the old man. He had never hurt me in any way. I didn't want his gold. I think it was his eye! Yes! He had a pale, blue eye, the eye of a vulture. Whenever I looked at it, my blood became cold; and so, very slowly, I decided to kill the old man and escape from the eye for ever.

You are thinking, I know, that I am mad. But madmen are not clever. And see how cleverly I prepared my plan! Every day that week I was so kind to the old man! And every night of that week, at about midnight, I opened his door very, very quietly. First I put my dark lantern through the opening of the door. The lantern was closed, and so no light came out of it, none at all. Then slowly, very slowly, I put my head inside the opening. I took sixty long minutes just to put my head inside. Would a madman have worked so carefully? And when my head was inside the room, I opened the lantern carefully and a thin ray of light fell onto the vulture eye. But the eye was always closed, so I could not do the work. You see, I did not hate the man; it was only the eye that I hated.

On the eighth night I started opening the door even more carefully. I was feeling calm and strong. There I was, opening his door, and he did not even know that I was there! I almost laughed at the idea. And perhaps, at that moment, he heard me, because he suddenly moved in his bed. But I did not move away. I knew that he could not see the opening of the door, so I continued pushing it open, slowly and quietly.

But the eye was always closed, so I could not do the work.

When my head was in the room, I tried to open the lantern but my thumb slipped and I made a noise. Immediately, the man sat up in bed and shouted, 'Who's there?'

I said nothing. For an hour I just stood there, without moving, and he sat in his bed, listening. Then he made a soft noise, a noise which I recognized. It was the noise of terror, the terror of death. I knew the sound because I had made it myself, many times, in the deep of the night, when all the world was asleep. I felt sorry for the old man, but I laughed silently. I knew that he had been awake since the first noise, and his fear had grown and grown. Death had entered his room, and now the shadow of death lay all around him. He could neither see me nor hear me, but he could *feel* my head inside his room.

I opened the lantern a little and a thin ray of light fell on his eye. It was open, and as I looked at it, I became angry. I could see it clearly, a horrible, pale blue eye that turned my blood cold. I could see nothing of the man's face or body, just his eye.

And then I heard a sound. Hadn't I told you that my hearing was excellent? I knew the sound. It was the beating of the old man's heart. It grew louder and quicker. Yes, louder and louder with every minute. The old man's terror must have been very great. And now a new terror came to me – a neighbour might hear the noise of this beating heart! The old man's time had come!

I opened the lantern fully and ran into the room. He shouted once – but only once because I pulled him to the floor and pulled the heavy bed over him. For many minutes the heart continued to beat, but then it stopped. The old

I pulled the old man to the floor.

man was dead. I put my hand on his heart and held it there for many minutes. There was no life in him at all. Now his eye would not trouble me again.

Perhaps you are still thinking that I am mad. You will not, when I tell you of the clever way I hid the body. First,

I cut it into pieces. I cut off the head and the arms and the legs. I then took up three boards from the wooden floor, and hid the body underneath. Finally, I replaced the wooden boards with great care. Now no human eye – not even *his* – would see anything wrong. There was nothing to see – not even any blood. A bowl had caught it all – ha! ha!

When I finished, it was four o'clock and it was still dark. There was a knock at the front door. Calmly, because I knew I had nothing to fear, I opened the door. Three policemen came in. They had come because a neighbour had reported a loud shout coming from the house.

I welcomed the policemen and asked them to come in. I explained that it was I who had shouted, in a dream. The old man, I said, was away in the country. I took them round the house and asked them to search it well. Then I took them to the old man's room and showed them all his things. I brought chairs into the room and invited them to sit down and rest a while. Calmly, I put my own chair on the place where I had hidden his body.

The policemen seemed happy. They could see from the way I spoke that all was well. They continued talking, but I began to get tired. My head ached, and there was a ringing noise in my ears. I wanted the men to go away, but they continued to talk. The ringing became louder and clearer. And then I realized that the noise was *not* in my ears.

I became very pale, and started talking more loudly. But the noise became louder too. What could I do? It was a low, soft sound, like the sound made by a watch when it is covered in cotton. I spoke more loudly. The noise became louder too. Why, oh why, didn't the men go away? I walked up

And now the noise was louder, louder, LOUDER!

and down the room. I became angry, I argued, I threw the chair onto the floor. But the noise continued to grow louder, louder than every noise I made. And the men went on talking and smiling. Was it possible that they hadn't heard the terrible noise? No! no! They heard! *They knew!* They were only pretending that they hadn't heard the noise! I was sure of this – I still am – and I hated their smiling faces. I felt that I must scream or die! And now, again, the noise was louder, louder, *louder*!

'Stop!' I shouted. 'Stop pretending that you cannot hear it! Yes, I did it! Pull up the floorboards here! here, here! – it is the beating of his horrible heart!'

GLOSSARY

advice what you say to help people

alcohol liquid in drinks like beer and whisky that can make people drunk

anger the feeling when you are angry

axe a tool for cutting trees and wood

basket a kind of strong bag

believe to think that something is true or right

board *(n)* a long thin flat piece of wood

brick a small hard block which is used for building walls

candle a round stick of wax which gives light when it burns

cellar a room in the ground under a house

chest the front part of the top of the body

chime the sound of a bell in a clock

cloak *(n)* a wide loose coat without sleeves

coffin the box in which a dead person is put

crack *(n)* a thin hole where something is broken; *(v)* to break open

cruel not kind; bringing pain or trouble to someone

double the stakes in gambling, to play for twice the amount of money

dragon a big dangerous animal with fire in its mouth, which lives only in stories

evil very bad, very wrong

gambling playing games of chance (e.g. cards, roulette) for money

gate a 'door' in a wall outside

gloom a feeling of deep sadness and hopelessness

hang to kill someone by holding him above the ground with a rope around his neck

heaven the home of God, where many people believe they will
  go when they die

hell the place where bad people go when they die

horrible making you very frightened

horror a feeling of great fear or dislike

huge very big

imagination making pictures in your mind

imagine to have a picture of something in your mind

lantern a light in a closed glass box

mad with a sick mind

mask a cover that is put over the face to hide it

masked ball a big party for dancing, where all the people wear
  masks

masque an old kind of play in the theatre with music and
  dancing

mind *(n)* the part of you that thinks, feels and remembers

nervous afraid, worried

outlined showing the line or shape of something

paint *(v)* to make a picture using different colours and a brush

pale with little colour in the face

passage a narrow way in a building which leads to other rooms

plaster something soft and wet which is put over bricks and
  which hardens to make the wall flat and straight

pleasure a strong feeling of enjoyment

plunge to push something in hard and suddenly

ray a thin line of light

rope very thick strong string

servant somebody who works in another person's house

sleeve the part of a shirt, coat, etc. that covers the arm

slip *(v)* to move suddenly by accident, and fall or almost fall

socket (eye socket) the hole in the head where the eye is

sword a very long sharp knife, used for fighting

tears *(n)* drops of water that come from the eye when you cry

terror very great fear

throw to move your arm quickly to send something through the air

vault a room under the ground of an old house or church

violet *(adj)* a bluish-purple colour

vulture a large bird that eats dead animals

weak not strong

whisper *(n)* the sound of a voice speaking very softly and quietly

wine an alcoholic drink made from grapes (small green or purple fruit)

ACTIVITIES

Before Reading

1 **Read the back cover and the introduction on the first page of the book. Are these sentences true (T) or false (F)?**

1 These stories are about real people and real places.
2 These stories are about strange things that happen in the mind.
3 After Lady Madeleine's death, her brother feels sad but peaceful.
4 The people at Prince Prospero's ball are having fun, not thinking about death.
5 These stories are good to read when you are feeling ill, unhappy or frightened.

2 **Here are the titles of the five stories. Which of the five things below belongs to each story? Can you guess?**

an axe / a blue eye / a strange book / a large black clock / a game of cards

The Fall of the House of Usher _____
The Black Cat _____
The Masque of the Red Death _____
William Wilson _____
The Tell-Tale Heart _____

ACTIVITIES

While Reading

Read *The Fall of the House of Usher*. **Choose the best question-word for these questions, and then answer them.**

Who / Where / What / Why

1 . . . did Roderick Usher write to the narrator?
2 . . . was becoming weaker and thinner each day?
3 . . . did they put the Lady Madeleine's coffin?
4 . . . did the narrator walk around the room during the storm?
5 . . . did the narrator do to make Usher calmer?
6 . . . did Usher realize from the sounds that he had heard?
7 . . . stood outside the door of the narrator's room?
8 . . . happened to the House of Usher?

Read *The Black Cat*. **Are these sentences true (T) or false (F)? Rewrite the false ones with the correct information.**

1 The narrator liked animals more than people.
2 Pluto the dog was the narrator's favourite animal.
3 When Pluto bit the narrator, he cut one of its legs off.
4 The shape of a cat appeared on the bedroom wall.
5 The new cat looked the same as Pluto in every way.
6 The narrator killed his wife with an axe.
7 After he killed his wife, the narrator slept badly.
8 The police found the living woman and the dead cat together behind the wall.

Read *The Masque of the Red Death*. Then answer these questions.

1 Who was *not* afraid of the Red Death?
2 Who did Prince Prospero invite to his castle?
3 Why could nobody enter or escape from the castle?
4 What were the colours of the seven rooms in the castle?
5 What was against the wall in the last room?
6 What did people notice while the clock was chiming midnight?
7 What was the stranger wearing?
8 How did the Prince feel when he saw the stranger?
9 Why didn't anyone want to touch the stranger?
10 What happened when the stranger turned and looked at the Prince?
11 What was inside the stranger's clothes and mask?
12 What was left in the castle when the clock stopped chiming?

Read *William Wilson*. Then match these halves of sentences to make a paragraph of seven sentences.

1 The narrator had to leave Oxford for Europe . . .
2 But in every city that he visited . . .
3 When he had evil plans, . . .
4 At first the narrator obeyed Wilson's orders, . . .
5 This made him feel brave and strong . . .
6 At last, at a party in Rome, the narrator took his sword . . .
7 But when he looked at his enemy's face, . . .

8 the other Wilson stopped them.

9 because everyone knew that he was a cheat at cards.

10 he saw that it was the same as his own.

11 and he thought that he could break away from his enemy.

12 the other William Wilson appeared.

13 and killed the other man.

14 but then he began drinking heavily.

Read *The Tell-Tale Heart*. Here are some untrue sentences about it. Change them into true sentences.

1 Because of his disease the narrator had terrible hearing.

2 The old man had once hurt the narrator in some way.

3 The narrator decided to kill the old man because of his gold.

4 The narrator took thirty minutes to put his head inside the old man's room.

5 The old man could see and hear the narrator in his room.

6 The narrator felt sorry when he saw the old man's eye.

7 The narrator pulled a heavy table on top of the old man.

8 He hid the old man's dead body behind the wall.

9 The policemen came to the house because a neighbour had seen a strange man there.

10 The narrator told the police that the old man was away in hospital.

11 When the narrator spoke more loudly, the noise in the room became quieter.

12 The noise in the room was the old man's watch.

ACTIVITIES

After Reading

1 Imagine that the narrator in *The Fall of the House of Usher* wrote to his wife during his visit. Use the linking words below to complete his letter.

although / and / but / but / since / so / when / which / who

Dear Sarah

I have been here for a week now. Usher was pleased to see me, _____ he has changed so much since our last meeting. He has a strange disease, _____ makes him very thin, pale and nervous. _____ I arrived, we have spent a lot of time together. I try to help him, _____ his sadness is too deep, _____ sometimes I am frightened by his fantastic ideas.

   Two days ago Usher's sister Madeleine died, _____ I must stay here a little longer. _____ I hate this house of gloom and madness, I must help my friend, _____ needs me very much.

_____ he feels stronger, I will leave this terrible place for ever. With love, Nathaniel

2 The policemen who found the black cat wrote a report about their visit to the house. Put these sentences in order, joining the parts where necessary, in order to make their report.

1 He knocked on one of the cellar walls with his stick, . . .
2 the owner took us down to the cellar.
3 and on top of her head there was a black cat with one eye.

4 so we got ready to leave.

5 On the 7th July we went to 51 Baker Street.

6 The cat was making the terrible sound that we had heard.

7 and suddenly we heard a sound from behind the wall.

8 Soon we found the dead body of a woman, . . .

9 After we had searched the rooms upstairs, . . .

10 We found nothing unusual there . . .

11 but then it became a loud and terrible scream.

12 Then the owner began to tell us how well built the house was.

13 We began to pull the wall down.

14 At first it was a soft cry, . . .

3 **Imagine that Prince Prospero, in *The Masque of the Red Death*, speaks to the stranger just before he dies. Complete their conversation. (Use as many words as you like.)**

PRINCE: _____?

STRANGER: You know who I am.

PRINCE: How _____? The gates _____.

STRANGER: I do not need a key to pass through a locked gate.

PRINCE: _____ at once! Or I _____.

STRANGER: I will not leave. And your sword cannot hurt me.

PRINCE: But what _____?

STRANGER: I have many names, but tonight I am called the Red Death.

PRINCE: Why _____?

STRANGER: Because, Prince Prospero, it is time for you to die.

4 Who, or what, was the other William Wilson? Which of these answers do you think is the best explanation?

1 a real person – who happens to look just like the narrator
2 a different part of the narrator's own mind
3 somebody that the narrator imagines, in a waking dream
4 the good side of the narrator's character
5 a kind of ghost

5 Here are four passages from Wilson's diary. Complete them with the words below (use each word once), and then say who wrote each passage – the 'good' or the 'bad' Wilson.

cards, caught, cheat, cheating, clever, destroy, enough, evil, gambler, make, mine, pleasure, secret, should, sleeve, stop, stupid, thief, where, wife

1 I no longer play cards. I am known to be a _____, which is no better than a _____. Once, when I tried to win a lot of money by _____, I was _____ and told to leave Oxford at once. But the man that I tried to _____ was saved.

2 At Oxford I was a clever and successful _____. It was an easy way to _____ money. I used special _____, which I hid inside my _____. I only played with _____ people, but sadly, one day I was caught, and so had to leave England.

3 Tonight the Duke Di Broglio's _____ has agreed to meet me in a room _____ we can be alone. She is young, beautiful, and not very _____ – and tonight she will be _____! I shall fight anybody who tries to _____ me.

4 I spend my life searching for _____. Tonight I have planned a _____ meeting with the Duke's wife. She is beautiful, but not clever _____ to recognize an _____ man when she sees one. Somebody _____ warn her about me.

6 In *The Tell-Tale Heart* a neighbour talks to the police (see page 53). Put their conversation in the correct order and write in the speakers' names. The policeman speaks first (number 7).

1 _____ 'This old man – do you know him?'
2 _____ 'Well, there was a terrible noise tonight from the house next door – like a great shout or a scream.'
3 _____ 'Strange? In what way?'
4 _____ 'Hmm. I think I should go next door and ask a few questions. Thank you for telling us about this.'
5 _____ 'I'm not sure – about two o'clock perhaps.'
6 _____ 'I went to the window and looked out. I didn't see anyone, but there was a light in the old man's room.'
7 _____ 'Now, sir, what's the problem?'
8 _____ 'So what did you do then?'
9 _____ 'He talks to himself – and he has really wild eyes.'
10 _____ 'Oh yes – he's a very nice man. A younger man lives in the house too – but he's a bit strange.'
11 _____ 'No, just one. But after that there was a loud bang – like something heavy falling to the floor.'
12 _____ 'Two o'clock. I see. And were there any more screams?'
13 _____ 'What time did you hear this scream?'

7 Perhaps this is what some of the characters in the stories were
   thinking. Which five characters are they (one from each story),
   and what is happening in the story at this moment?

   1 Oh my God! Who is *that*? He looks really terrible. And all
      that blood! I don't think that's very funny. How can we
      enjoy ourselves with that in front of us? And how did he
      get in? Somebody will have to tell the Prince . . .

   2 What's happening? Something woke me up. I can't see
      anything, but I know there's something there. I'm so
      afraid. I'm listening and listening – it's dark and quiet, but
      I can feel something terrible, something frightening . . .

   3 Now the wall is finished, he thinks he's safe – but he's
      wrong. He didn't see me climb in here with the body. I'll
      just sit here and wait until somebody comes – and then I'll
      open my mouth and scream . . .

   4 Soon it will end. On this wild night I will at last be free –
      free to search for my brother, and take him with me. One
      more push, and this wood will break. Then the door, and
      up the stairs. You cannot escape me now, brother . . .

   5 I don't know what's wrong with me tonight. I must have
      unlucky cards – I've *always* won before when I've played
      against him. Mustn't look worried. Have another glass of
      wine. He'll make a mistake soon, and then I'll win all my
      money back . . .

8 Look at these adjectives and nouns from the story. Make three pairs of words – an adjective plus a noun – to suit each story. You can use words more than once.

Adjectives:

dark	mysterious
deep	sad
evil	silent
fantastic	strange
frightening	terrible
ghostly	violent
loud	wild

Nouns:

anger	gloom	sadness
animal	house	scream
castle	idea	sound
disease	murder	storm
face	person	stranger
fear	plan	
feeling	pleasure	

9 Imagine that these stories appear in the newspapers. Here are some headlines for the stories. Which headlines go with which stories? Which headlines do you prefer? Why?

FANTASTIC PARTY ENDS IN DEATH

HOUSE DISAPPEARS IN STORM

KILLER HIDES BODY, THEN TELLS POLICE

CAT CALLS POLICE TO BODY

STRANGE DEATHS OF BROTHER AND SISTER

IS THIS THE MOST EVIL MAN IN EUROPE?

ANIMAL-LOVER ARRESTED FOR MURDER

MAN KILLS ENEMY — AND MURDERS SELF

THE RICH AND THE CRUEL PUNISHED AT LAST

'I CAN'T ESCAPE TERRIBLE SOUND,' MAD KILLER TELLS POLICE

10 Which story did you find most frightening? Why?

ABOUT THE AUTHOR

Edgar Allan Poe was born in 1809 in Boston, USA. His parents died when he was young, and he went to live with the Allan family in Richmond. He spent a year at university, and then two years in the army. In 1831 he moved to Baltimore, where he lived with his aunt and his cousin Virginia. For the next few years life was difficult; he wrote stories and sold them to magazines, but it brought him little money. But he did find happiness with Virginia, whom he married in 1836.

From 1838 to 1844 Poe lived in Philadelphia, where he wrote some of his most famous stories, such as *The Fall of the House of Usher* and *The Murders in the Rue Morgue*, and worked for different magazines. Then he moved to New York City, where his poem *The Raven* soon made him famous. But Virginia died in 1847, and Poe began drinking heavily. He tried to kill himself in 1848, and died the following year.

Poe is best known for his horror stories, but they are just a small part of his work. He can be called the father of the modern detective story, because of his story *The Murders in the Rue Morgue* – the first story to show how the detective thinks. (The Mystery Writers of America give a prize called an 'Edgar' to the writer of the best mystery each year.) He wrote poetry, funny stories, and stories about time travel – a kind of early science fiction. He also wrote about other writers of his time. But to most people the name Edgar Allan Poe means stories of death and madness, horror and ghosts.

OXFORD BOOKWORMS LIBRARY

Classics • Crime & Mystery • Factfiles • Fantasy & Horror
Human Interest • Playscripts • Thriller & Adventure
True Stories • World Stories

The OXFORD BOOKWORMS LIBRARY provides enjoyable reading in English, with a wide range of classic and modern fiction, non-fiction, and plays. It includes original and adapted texts in seven carefully graded language stages, which take learners from beginner to advanced level. An overview is given on the next pages.

All Stage 1 titles are available as audio recordings, as well as over eighty other titles from Starter to Stage 6. All Starters and many titles at Stages 1 to 4 are specially recommended for younger learners. Every Bookworm is illustrated, and Starters and Factfiles have full-colour illustrations.

The OXFORD BOOKWORMS LIBRARY also offers extensive support. Each book contains an introduction to the story, notes about the author, a glossary, and activities. Additional resources include tests and worksheets, and answers for these and for the activities in the books. There is advice on running a class library, using audio recordings, and the many ways of using Oxford Bookworms in reading programmes. Resource materials are available on the website <www.oup.com/elt/gradedreaders>.

The *Oxford Bookworms Collection* is a series for advanced learners. It consists of volumes of short stories by well-known authors, both classic and modern. Texts are not abridged or adapted in any way, but carefully selected to be accessible to the advanced student.

You can find details and a full list of titles in the *Oxford Bookworms Library Catalogue* and *Oxford English Language Teaching Catalogues*, and on the website <www.oup.com/elt/gradedreaders>.

THE OXFORD BOOKWORMS LIBRARY GRADING AND SAMPLE EXTRACTS

STARTER • 250 HEADWORDS

present simple – present continuous – imperative –
can/cannot, must – *going to* (future) – simple gerunds …

Her phone is ringing – but where is it?

Sally gets out of bed and looks in her bag. No phone. She looks under the bed. No phone. Then she looks behind the door. There is her phone. Sally picks up her phone and answers it. *Sally's Phone*

STAGE 1 • 400 HEADWORDS

… past simple – coordination with *and, but, or* –
subordination with *before, after, when, because, so* …

I knew him in Persia. He was a famous builder and I worked with him there. For a time I was his friend, but not for long. When he came to Paris, I came after him – I wanted to watch him. He was a very clever, very dangerous man. *The Phantom of the Opera*

STAGE 2 • 700 HEADWORDS

… present perfect – *will* (future) – *(don't) have to, must not, could* –
comparison of adjectives – simple *if* clauses – past continuous –
tag questions – *ask/tell* + infinitive …

While I was writing these words in my diary, I decided what to do. I must try to escape. I shall try to get down the wall outside. The window is high above the ground, but I have to try. I shall take some of the gold with me – if I escape, perhaps it will be helpful later. *Dracula*

STAGE 3 • 1000 HEADWORDS

... should, may – present perfect continuous – *used to* – past perfect –
causative – relative clauses – indirect statements ...

Of course, it was most important that no one should see
Colin, Mary, or Dickon entering the secret garden. So Colin
gave orders to the gardeners that they must all keep away
from that part of the garden in future. ***The Secret Garden***

STAGE 4 • 1400 HEADWORDS

... past perfect continuous – passive (simple forms) –
would conditional clauses – indirect questions –
relatives with *where/when* – gerunds after prepositions/phrases ...

I was glad. Now Hyde could not show his face to the world
again. If he did, every honest man in London would be proud
to report him to the police. ***Dr Jekyll and Mr Hyde***

STAGE 5 • 1800 HEADWORDS

... future continuous – future perfect –
passive (modals, continuous forms) –
would have conditional clauses – modals + perfect infinitive ...

If he had spoken Estella's name, I would have hit him. I was so
angry with him, and so depressed about my future, that I could
not eat the breakfast. Instead I went straight to the old house.
Great Expectations

STAGE 6 • 2500 HEADWORDS

... passive (infinitives, gerunds) – advanced modal meanings –
clauses of concession, condition

When I stepped up to the piano, I was confident. It was as if I
knew that the prodigy side of me really did exist. And when I
started to play, I was so caught up in how lovely I looked that
I didn't worry how I would sound. ***The Joy Luck Club***

BOOKWORMS · FANTASY & HORROR · STAGE 3

Frankenstein

MARY SHELLEY

Retold by Patrick Nobes

Victor Frankenstein thinks he has found the secret of life. He takes parts from dead people and builds a new 'man'. But this monster is so big and frightening that everyone runs away from him – even Frankenstein himself!

The monster is like an enormous baby who needs love. But nobody gives him love, and soon he learns to hate. And, because he is so strong, the next thing he learns is how to kill …

BOOKWORMS · CRIME & MYSTERY · STAGE 3

The Last Sherlock Holmes Story

MICHAEL DIBDIN

Retold by Rosalie Kerr

For fifty years after Dr Watson's death, a packet of papers, written by the doctor himself, lay hidden in a locked box. The papers contained an extraordinary report of the case of Jack the Ripper and the horrible murders in the East End of London in 1888. The detective, of course, was the great Sherlock Holmes – but why was the report kept hidden for so long?

This is the story that Sir Arthur Conan Doyle never wrote. It is a strange and frightening tale . . .